W/D

ity L

wo weeks

per week o
charged c

Sculpture in Black Ice

BREDA SULLIVAN

salmonpoetry

More Poetry by Breda Sullivan

A Smell of Camphor (Salmon, 1992)
After the Ball (Salmon, 1998)

for my siblings

Seán Ó Leocháin, Madeline Christie, Joseph Ducke

with love

Published in 2004 by
Salmon Publishing Ltd.,
Cliffs of Moher, County Clare, Ireland
Website: www.salmonpoetry.com
email: info@salmonpoetry.com

ISBN 1 903392 43 8

Cover photography: Jack Dodd
Cover design & typesetting: Siobhán Hutson

Salmon Publishing gratefully acknowleges the
support of The Arts Council / An Chomhairle Ealaíon

'A clay pot sitting in the sun will always be a clay pot.
It has to go through the white heat of the furnace
to become porcelain.'
MILDRED WITTE STOUVEN

Acknowledgments

Acknowledgments are due to the following publications in which some of these poems were previously published:

Journals: *Poetry Ireland Review, Cyphers, Books Ireland, Acorn, Incognito, Force 10, The Stinging Fly, Stroan, Edgeworth Papers, Connacht Tribune, Longford Leader, Riposte, Figments, The Palace Papers, Education Today Literary Supplement, Virtual Writer,* and *The Envelope.*

Anthologies: *Six for Gold, Women's Work Anthologies, Heartland, Beneath the Moat 11, Reaching Out, Heart of Kerry, Jumping the Bus Queue, A Mother Is...*(U.K.), *This Moment in Time* (U.K.), and *What Makes The World Go Round?* (U.K.).

The Light in my Window: First Prize National Women's Poetry Competition 1998.

The Long Winter: First Prize K.I.S.S. (Kerry International Summer School) Poetry Competition 1995.

The Lost Child (a version): First Prize Clogh Writers Poetry Competition 1997.

Baby Breath: Second Prize Athlone River Festival Poetry Competition 1996. Third Prize Open Section Scottish International Poetry Competition.

Roses and Snow: Second Prize Cootehill Literary Awards 1998.

To the Heinrich Böll Committee, Achill Island, a special thanks for my residency in Böll Cottage, November 2001, where this collection was compiled.

Thanks to:

Paul Perry for his help during his term as writer-in-residence in Longford.

Áine Miller for her advice with the manuscript.

Susan Connolly, Josephine McCabe, June Murphy for reading and responding to the manuscript.

Granard Writers' Group for their encouragement and support.

Contents

1

Balloons

in the silence
of a white room
she came to me

the child
clutching a bunch
of black balloons

one by one
I ease the strings
from her thin fingers

Cylinders

Mother's birthday present
always the same:
a jar of coffee,
a packet of goldgrain biscuits
half covered
with milk chocolate.

Two cylinders
in fancy paper:
luxuries she enjoyed
but never afforded,
bought with pennies
we sacrificed for weeks.

Home,
we open the door:
strange aroma of coffee;
we shrug off school-bags,
smile at each other,
rewarded.

Her Telephone

a bean tin
on the window sill
outside

flung across the wall
it clattered on the concrete
next door alerting Mrs. Brown

she chatted with my mother
through the hedge-gap
until the cold sudden rain

or a child calling *Mammy
the bread smells burning*
chased them indoors

Sunday Excursion

for Eilis and Marguerite

Under a bridge
the train whistles,
spring well flashes past.

Faces press
to the glass
anticipating
cousins waving.
We wave back.

The train s–l–o–w–s,
changes chant,
puffs to a halt.

From the luggage rack
my father hands down:
buckets and spades,
duileasg, a Lydon's cake,
sticks of Galway rock.

On the platform
my sister pauses,
kicks Salthill sand

from her sandals;
the boys grumble.
My mother says:
*I'll shake hands
with the tea-pot.*

The Light in my Window

for Barry, Troy, Eimear, Declan

i

I remember
the early years
of anticipation

imagining
how I would tell him
the good news

planning
a special supper
before the fire

choosing to tell him
at that moment
I lit the candle between us

picturing
on his face
joy and wonder.

ii

At the clinic
in Mullingar
our candle was snuffed.

In silence
we drove home
to mourn.

I opened
the wardrobe,
wore black clothes,

went to school:
smiled at my pupils,
talked to colleagues;

while a she-wolf
howled
across the tundra.

iii

We completed
application forms,
answered

intimate questions,
strangers
inspected our home.

iv

At last,
I discard
my black garb.

With strands of colour
plucked from the light in my window
weave a long flowing robe.

I open the door wide,
step outside
into a sun-bright garden

and I know
the four children
racing towards me

mine
beyond flesh
beyond blood.

Noon

for Basil

Hoovering a thousand needles from the carpet
a small price to pay
for the scent of pine at Christmas time.

Sitting in the quiet of the flickering firelight
I walk once again
a fragrant forest path in Glenmalure.

The children race ahead chasing imaginary wolves
or squealing with fright
at the scurry of small creatures in the undergrowth.

Their father and I stroll behind
arm in arm or hand in hand
and sunset is a long way off.

Sons

i—*Sunday Lunch*

The chicken
has too many
legs today

it was
a stupid thing
to cook

the sunday after
my son
went away.

ii—*Trust*

I watch my son toss
his baby daughter
ceiling-wards.

In those seconds
when gravity might win
she squeals with glee

freefalls and lands
safely in her father's
waiting hands.

iii—*Home*

It wasn't his moving out
to a flat
the Saturday after
his eighteenth birthday
that hurt,
but when he called
later that evening
and I gave him
a pillow, sheets, duvet,
a clock to waken him
and he asked:
Who'll drive me home?

Daughter

knows
what I can't
ever know

life beginning
secret
in her womb

pangs of birth
her child's
first cry

his face
an image
of her own

Now

My grandson
is sleeping.

I'm glad
he wasn't born
decades ago.

He could be
in America,
adopted by
a wealthy family.

His mother
in a Magdalen laundry,
labouring for life.

I the one who
sentenced her.

Ecce Homo

after a painting by Titian, National Gallery, Dublin

The ropes I notice most,
wound round and round
his criss-crossed wrists,
hands limp. The purple cloak.
Thorns nail and halo the head
bowed, eyes downcast.

Dawn from Bethlehem Hotel:
over the West Bank
an oyster shell opens
gold pink mauve blue
(that incredible cloudless blue)
the sun a fiery pearl in its throat.

A coach across the border:
Palestinian police,
Israeli soldiers:
boys in uniform
but their guns can kill.

Jerusalem. City of Peace.
Ancient narrow streets.
An Arab boy—beautiful—
no more than nine or ten,
olive skin, dark liquid eyes,
raises his hand and cries:
Praise Allah.
A hawker calls:
Two Rosaries, one dollar.
Noticing a nun in our group
his call becomes excited, insistent:
Twelve Rosaries, five dollars.

Our native guide hurries us on
before shops open and this becomes
a crowded, commercial street.

Via Dolorosa.

Ecce Homo Arch.

The guide selects
the first four
to shoulder the cross
and so begins
our Via Crucis.
Shaded streets
but already it is hot.

We pause at each station,
touch walls made holy
by history and two millennia
of pilgrim hands.

Jesus meets His mother.

At home, our eldest son worries for our safety.
Every day, media reports of more unrest
in Jerusalem and the West Bank.
More killings.

Our first grandson struggles
for life
in Sligo General Hospital.
Nativity with no Advent.

Lord, that he may live.
Forgive my first black thought
maybe he will die. A neat solution
to an unplanned life.

Armed Israeli soldiers.
Each pilgrim eye seeks
the grey clad figure
of our bishop.
Our guide shepherds us;
progress reluctant
for this journey
has one end:

Golgotha.

for Bishop Colm O'Reilly and fellow pilgrims
to the Holy Land October 2000

Walk

for Barry eile

I wheel my grandbaby
under trees
to Roosky Lock,
a quiet road
between the Shannon
and the N4.

Noisy trucks
turn his head,
I look
the other way
to the river
and silence.

Story

for Emma, Barry, Jack

House silent,
grandchildren gone.

Their parents
tug at my sleeve

climb on my knee
open the book

ask me to read
the story again.

2

The Lost Child

I place a tumbler
on my bedside locker.

I place it
on white lace

crocheted
by my mother.

In sleep I dream
I am weeping.

My sister is lost
and I am weeping.

Over and over
I call her name.

Hands cupped
about my mouth

I call her name;
snail home.

By the window
my mother

crochets white lace.
In the moonlight

the tumbler by my bed
brims with tears.

Man cleans range
before he lights
new day's fire,
poking and raking
familiar morning sounds.
Strange clink. Blackened
coins drop one by one
from grate into ash pan,
ash rises; sudden little puffs grey
as face of woman in bed upstairs,
silence more terrible
than lifting range lid,
flinging coins into flame,
money doesn't grow on bushes;
grief far into night.

At dusk the lost child,
daisy dress dishevelled,
pocket heavy with coins.

Warned often
at home, at school:
*Do not talk
to strangers*.

Never told
not to hold
the hand
of a neighbour.

Baby Breath

i.m. James Butler

The father opened the door, showed me in
through the crowded subdued kitchen.

The mother lay on one bed,
the infant in his carry-cot on the other.

I shook hands with both parents,
murmured my sympathy;

the mother's hand clammy and limp,
the father's firm and strong;

their baby a bluebell
in his hand-knitted suit.

Awkwardly, I stood there,
unsure what I should do:

no holy water to sprinkle,
no crossing of me and the child,

no place to kneel, no rosary beads,
no unison of Hail Marys.

I wished one of their own would come
and I could mimic him.

He looks peaceful the father said.
Very peaceful I agreed.

Peaceful as though sleeping
but no rise and fall of chest.

I wanted to raise him up,
open him like a Russian doll,

discard shell after shell
until I held on my palm

the innermost nut:
the seed of his breathing.

Bog Cotton in the Wind

i

The family next door
went to their granny's in Achill
the Easter before I was seven.

I remember:
closed windows,
a closed door,
and moping
about our garden
on my own.

The evening they returned
my mother went next door alone.

I hear her key turn,
see her strange face,
and my father
looking at her
over the evening paper,
looking at her
over his reading glasses,
until at last he said *Marie*
and she shook her head
and whispered—

meningitis.

ii

I don't want her to be in heaven.
I want her here. Now.
I want her to tell me about Achill
and her Granny talking Irish.
I want to walk to school with her
tomorrow like always.

I want to tell her
I got my new sandals
for First Communion.
I want to show them to her
after school.
I want to play with her.
I want us to practice
our Irish dancing.
We have to.
Miss Rowan said.
What about First Communion?
I want us to make it together
like we were supposed to.

iii

We've come to see Jenny-Jo,
Jenny-Jo, Jenny-Jo,
we've come to see Jenny-Jo.

You can't see her now.

Jenny-Jo is sick in bed,
sick in bed, sick in bed,
Jenny-Jo is sick in bed.

You can't see her now.

We've come to see Jenny-Jo,
Jenny-Jo, Jenny-Jo,
we've come to see Jenny-Jo,

You can't see her now.

Jenny-Jo is dead in bed,
dead in bed, dead in bed,
Jenny-Jo is dead in bed.

You can't see her now.

iv

You are standing
on green lino
on our kitchen floor,
rocking Joe to sleep
in his pram.
My mother
peeps at the baby,
gives you a penny.
Heads together

we sit
in my father's
big armchair,
your hair
short and dark,
mine fair, waving
to my waist.
We look at
coloured pictures

turn a page.
We look into each other's face:
yours pale, oval,
mine round, freckled.
It is tea-time.
From next door
a knock
on the wall
and you are gone.

v

The first morning
in my new class
I studied the picture
above the nun's head.

Two children
bent to pick flowers

close to the cliff edge.
Behind them an angel
with great wings
outstretched
to protect.
Then we knelt.

All together we said
our morning prayer:
Oh angel of God
my guardian dear.
I bowed my head,
said nothing.

vi

We moved house. The girl next
door came to play in our garden.

I pushed her on the swing my father
made in the turf-shed doorway.

I never let her push me.
The years leap-frogged.

Secondary School. Leaving Cert.
Teacher Training College.

Marie a sob
in the wind from the bog,

a quiver
in long grass.

vii

At ballet class
it is not my daughter
I watch
doing pliés
at the barre.

I watch
a strange child
a frail child
a pale child
a dark haired child

plié, plié, plié.

viii

I never thought
to find you
in a tuft
of bog-cotton
blowing in the wind
in my six year old
daughter's hand.

Bog cotton
that honeymoon day.
The shock
of a dead sheep
on an Achill beach.
How the fleece

became buoyant and alive
with the incoming tide,
how the fleece
became a veil,
and the sheep
became a bride
or a First Communion child.

Last Requests

for Gearoid

When you last held your mother's hand
in the coronary care unit,
and asked, in that calm voice you have,
if she wanted for anything, she replied:

Yes. Put the bread I baked this morning
into the freezer. Strain the stock
simmering on the range. Post the letter
on the sideboard to your brother.

Nuala O'Brien 1918 – 1998

Roses and Snow

for Mona and Seamus

In this season of roses and mallow,
petunia spill from window boxes,
hanging baskets are wheels of colour.
Heat explodes. The first flash
cracks the sky to horizon. Thunder
is a pride of lions roaring and snarling
on the roof of my car. I turn up
the volume on the radio to hear
the current hit "Time to say Goodbye."
A duet. A downpour and I dash from car
park to hospital door, the great drops
a relief through my dress,
on my bare legs and sandalled feet.

I climb the stairs, bearing no gift
like a talisman. You can no longer eat,
drink or hold a book. Flowers bring
the knowledge of their burst from the earth
in annual resurrection. Your room is stripped
of get-well cards. I sit by your bed
watching blood drip through a thin tube
coiling to your hand. You are thinner
than a week ago. Restless, your limbs
bend, stretch, bend. *My feet and legs
feel as if I walked through snow
up to my knees* you manage to say.
Sudden pain rips your face.

Your free hand grips your abdomen.
I call the nurse, hold your hand
while you relax into a morphine sleep.
Half way down the stairs I return,

stand by your bed, needing
to look on your face once
more while you are still breathing.
Back home I wander the garden:
seek consolation in the pink of lupin,
the fresh scent of earth after rain.
In vain. This hot July day,
through a bleak white landscape I go
knee deep in drifts of snow.

Terry Bleakley 1949 - 1997

3

Spring Scouts

for Jennifer

If I don't look out the window
every morning,
I'll miss that late January day,

when yellow spiders scurry

along the bare branches
of the witch hazel,
and cling there.

Moonfire

Other plants I bought
for their foliage,
flowers, shape.

From Larry
in Abbeylara
garden centre

I bought
this dahlia
for its name.

The Begonia

in the hanging basket
outside the window
is beautiful.

Pendulous.
Apricot blooms big
as breakfast cups.

In the morning
when the light is right
I will take a photograph

before the flowers drop
like exotic spiders
onto the concrete.

Spring Rain

for Miho Nonaka

In my kitchen
on a farm

in north Westmeath,
an oriental girl

busy by the range;
silver saucepans simmer

with sea-weed soup
and see-through noodles

called, in Japanese,
spring rain.

She tests and tastes—another
dash of soy sauce for the stir-fry.

I set the table with great care,
go to the garden and pluck

a spray of fuchsia,
grey leaved senecio,

place them in a tiny vase
between white candles,

uncork a bottle of wine
and all is ready.

In my kitchen,
where usually stew

or spuds and cabbage bubble,
my friend from Tokyo

lifts from a saucepan
spring rain.

From Dugort Beach

To Böll cottage
I bring
a seagull's feather,
in a squat bottle
on the mantle
it resembles a quill.

A pocketful of white stones
I empty on the red window-sill,
gathered one by one
as my mother's voice echoed:
There's a godstone. Pick it up.
It'll bring you luck.

Silence

In my sister's house:
silence is three boys
gone to school,
a labrador sleeping.

In childhood, silence
was a valley
between giant storms.

Silence in my teaching days:
an empty school,
my footsteps echoing.

In my home now:
silence is a family grown,
a yellow rose rambling
to my window.

A Country Walk

In childhood yielded
bunches of cowslip,
shell of blackbird's egg,
mushrooms spilling
from father's upside down hat,
pockets bulging with chestnuts;
cans of blackberry, wild raspberry,
and bags heavy with crab apple
transformed by mother
into jams and jellies

to fill jars in rows
on shelves
at the back door.

Today, in middle age, yields
three plastic bottles
intact, two flattened,
pockets bulging with crisp bags,
cigarette packets,
blue baling twine,
a bag rattling with coke cans
plucked from the ditch,
in my arms
a hug of black plastic.

Endangered

for Emma

I bought books,
sat her on my lap
before the winter fire,
showed her pictures,
taught her words:
sky bird tree

flower snail butterfly.
Summer blew the fire out,
burst open windows and doors.
Together we escaped to the garden,
looked up at the sky

imitated bird flight.
She pointed to each *tee, tee*,
a snail, breakfasting on a lupin
leaf engrossed her,
with one finger she touched
fowa after *nice fowa*

plucked a petal,
treasured it indoors to grandad.
One foot on the step she paused,
looked up at me and asked:
Ganny, where butterfy?

Voyeur

He slipped the dress
over her head,
watched it slide
down her body

the black so black
against her whiteness.
In silence
he studied her.

His artist's hands ran
all over her,
coaxing the dress to fit
about breast waist hip.

On his knees before her
he smoothed the clingy cloth
across her belly
down her thighs.

He touched a bare knee,
stood up,
looked into her eyes,
lifted her as he would a child

carried her to the place
reserved for her
in the window of Longford's
Enable Ireland shop.

For all who work and shop in *Enable Ireland*, Longford

Winter Love

for Basil

Pot-bellied
white haired
I come to you

no make-up
fills the cracks
in my face

no foundation garment
holds my belly in
my breasts out

clad only
in my skin
I come to you

in your eyes
the same fire
ignites.

Nachtmusik

Bamberg 2001—for Ursula

Someone is playing
a piano,
over and over
the same piece,
fingers practice, perfect.
Notes spill with light
from a gap
between curtains,
spill with snow
across the courtyard
to where I stand
by a hotel window,
looking out
on red rooftops whiten,
and a rill of light, shafting
crotchets, quavers, minims,
that swarm the night
like snow.

4

Footprints

on my threshold stands
a child shivering

I hesitate   open the door
wide   invite him in

his wellington boots
muddy the floors

no matter how I try
I cannot erase

his black
footprints

Escape Routes

At art exhibitions
I buy pictures
of doors and windows,
hang them about my house
in every room and hall.

No matter where I am
when the exit seizes,
I will climb into a picture,
open a door or window
and escape.

Dear Vincent

Your *Bedroom at Arles*
hangs on a white wall
at the end of my bed
I change sheets
plump pillows
put fresh flowers in a jar
open the window
wait
for your step
on the stair
your sweat
filling the room
a sunflower
like thickly buttered bread
on the canvas
in your hand
while stars from your
Café Terrace at Night
implode in your eyes
and at Auvers
above a wheat field
the sky darkens
crows gather.

A Helium Balloon

Room stuffy
lecture boring

I watch a sunbeam
stage a dust dance

a red faced man opens
a window at the top

my head de-slots
from my neck

drifts   bobs
against the ceiling

floats to the window
and away.

Sun Worship

I follow the sun,
not in the usual way
winging towards the equator
to lie for two weeks
on a golden beach
my skin tingling with heat.

I follow the sun,
I shadow the earth's shift,
a polar creature
darkness and I are strangers, I lie
on a vast beach of ice
every pore open, absorbing light.

January Landscape

i

A strange
brightness
in the morning light

the landscape
white
with ice

and snow
deeper
than my ankle boots

a tangle of bushes
magical
with hoar frost

low sun
long tree shadows
over frozen flooded fields

in the distance
the river alive
and glimmering.

ii

One false step
and the road
is ice breaking

alone I flounder
in a frozen flood
in winter

the immaculate landscape
scarred
only by my footprints

my dropped mitten
a scarlet stain
in the snow.

Journey

Track steep, stones
sharp and loose.

On a bench
outside his log cabin

a white-bearded man
smokes a clay pipe.

I leave the track,
approach him and ask:

*Is this the way
to the summit?*

*Is it the summit
that's important?*

No I reply
it's the journey.

He goes inside,
returns with a paper bag:

a cheese sandwich
to sustain me.

Plucked from the Bog

i—*Reconstruction*

The therapy room
now
a waiting room

I sit with
my sore throat
eyes fixed
on a magazine

while the once
bare white walls
whisper my secrets.

ii—*Insomnia*

The mouse was back again

keeping her awake
sniffing packages

hidden in her attic

brown paper packages
tightly tied with string

disturbing decades' dust.

iii—*Shut-down*

The doorbell rings.
I sit statue still
glad no sound
from radio
or television
gives me existence.

Only when I hear
gravel crunch
do I steal
to my front room
peer through lace curtains
at another friend leave.

iv—*Framed*

A life-size image
hanging on the wall
happy smiling
in her framed world.

Thinking she had
substance
they took away
the frame.

v—*I think I am*

If I move
and I am not
there will be no movement.

If I speak
and I am not
there will be no sound.

If I weep
and I am not
there will be no tears.

I do not move.
I do not speak.
I do not weep.

vi—*The Field*

Imagine a field
square   green
grass close-cropped.

Imagine trying
to leave
this field.

At every turn
a gate
clangs shut.

Imagine standing
alone in this field
the barbed fence advancing.

vii—*Crystal*

I hold
a crystal bowl
between my palms.

It slips,
drops,
shatters

on hard tiles.
My head
a crystal bowl;

I hold it
between my palms,
tremble.

viii—*Psychotherapy*

There's no point
in driving up there
because even if I do
I'll never manage
to turn in the gate
and even if I do
I'll never manage
to drive to the house
and even if I do
I'll never manage
to switch off the engine
and even if I do
I'll never manage
to leave the car
and even if I do
I'll never manage
to walk to the door
and even if I do
I'll never manage
to press the bell
and even if I do
I'll never manage
to wait till the door opens
and even if I do
I'll never manage
to step inside
and even if I do
I'll never manage
to walk the long hall
and even if I do
I'll never manage
to enter that room
and even if I do
I'll never manage
to sit in that chair
until the silence

like a tin-opener
cuts a jagged hole
in my head
and up pops
this week's
jack-in-the-box
talking.

ix—*After Samhain*

I sink
into the black bog
of winter

no light
no sound
no chink
of a future spring

only the dark
damp silence
of millennia.

x—*November Nightmare*

The house
is submerged
in black ink

beyond the window
it presses black
against the glass

an octopus,
eyes like shattered crystal,
stares in at me

his tentacles
coil and uncoil
like springs

I close the curtains
dreading the sudden whack
the breaking of glass.

xi—*The Long Winter*

A black wind
screams
about my house

grabs beech trees
by the throat
and half throttles them

they claw
and struggle
to be free

at the end of the lawn
my evergreen shelter belt
is gap-toothed

a black wind
screams
about the yard

I cover my ears
and the hay-shed is a mangle
of contorted iron

tonight I lie
lulled
by silence

my eyes close
I drift
into sleep

while black snow
sifts
about my door.

xii—*Tenebrae*

I hold
my cupped hand
behind
the final flame

blow

ghosts
of dead candles
haunt
the air

smell

of molten wax
and then
nothing
only the tenebrous

dark.

xiii—*Plucked from the Bog*

You close the door,
I know I am safe.

Always at evening I come,
the uncurtained window
welcoming the dark

the lights of the town distant
as flung stars.

We sit, the table's length
between us. I place
at the centre tonight's token

a sculpture in black ice—
not carefully chiselled

until it became what I wanted,
but a sculpture in the way
a piece of oak is

plucked from the bog.
Slowly I begin to speak.

You listen with all
of your listening—
each word a black tear

dissolving. The sculpture now a black
pool, I take my leave of you.

My going a whisper
in the empty corridor,
down the long carpeted stairs.

Outside I look up
at the rectangle of light

that is your window.
Always at evening I will come
until the evening of evenings

when I place on your table
a sculpture carved in alabaster

so white
I will speak no word.
It will shed no tear.

xiv—*Cyclone*

after several
sunny days
the black bird
swoops
across my sky

his sharp beak
punctures the sun

like egg yolk
it slithers
down the sky
peeling with it
all my light

xv—*The Lost Years*

I fell asleep in springtime
to the nod of daffodil
my children's faces
like daisies
opening to the sun.

All summer I slept on
their squeals of laughter
the splash of atlantic water
filtering through the chinks
in my black dreaming.

Through autumn I slumbered
while they split conkers
kicked crisp leaves
blackberry stained their fingers
bit into the apple.

In winter I awoke
to a world of ice crystals
my children's faces
a memory
in the garden.

xvi—*Transition*

I have stayed too long
in the shadow of the past

raking the same
patch of earth

where the same
perennial weeds grow

picking old sores
lest they cease to bleed

scratching irritations
lest they cease to itch

rubbing scars
lest they fade.

Today the past
is a house deserted.

I walk from
room to room

feeling regret at what
might have been

sadness
at what was.

I place the key
on the uppermost step

descend the stairs,
pull the door

closed behind me.
I do not look back.

xvii—*Healing*

In sleep a wise old
woman came to me.

I named her Brigid
the name given to me

at birth. In silence
we sat facing,

her knees touched mine,
our hands like leaves

curled in our laps.
She closed her eyes,

sank deep
into that pool

of inner light. Slowly
her eyes opened, looked

into mine.

On a Garden Seat

In sudden sun
between april showers
they come to me

daisy crowned
two little girls
in white dresses

they fill my lap
with primrose,
dandelion, celandine

rain returns
the girls dissolve
like sugar children

the flowers rise—
a flock of birds
yellow, airborne.

W/D